# BIG
# Dinosaur
# Facts

Acknowledgements: p63(c) The Natural History Museum, p68(tr) NHPA/Stephen Dalton, p75(tl) Science Photo Library.

Published by Armadillo Books
An imprint of Bookmart Limited
Registered Number 2372865
Trading as Bookmart Limited
Desford Road
Enderby
Leicester
LE9 5AD

ISBN 1843220490

Produced for Bookmart by Planet Three Publishing Network,
10 Northburgh Street, London EC1V 0AT.

PLANET THREE PUBLISHING NETWORK

Printed in Singapore

# BIG
# Dinosaur
# Facts

ARMADILLO

# Contents

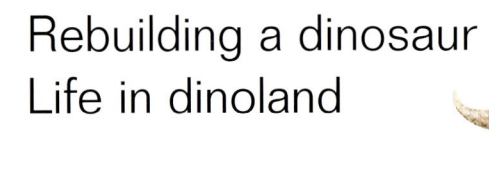

# Dinosaurs and us

## Dinosaur!

No other creatures have gripped our imaginations like the dinosaurs have. We are fascinated by them and we search endlessly for clues about their lives and how they died.

## Bone diggers

People who dig up and study dinosaur fossils are called 'palaeontologists'. Even tiny fragments of fossil bone are exciting when you know what to look for!

## Dino fans

For over 150 years, people have been interested in fossil dinosaurs and many have raced to find bigger and better skeletons. In film and television too, people have tried to bring dinosaurs back to life.

# What is a dinosaur?

## The new reptiles

Dinosaurs were a new kind of reptile that appeared on Earth 230 million years ago. They were different from other reptiles in a number of ways. Let's find out how.

**Herrerasaurus the dinosaur**

**Saurosuchus the reptile**

## Twinkle toes

The first dinosaurs stood on two legs and walked on their toes instead of on flat feet. This meant they could run faster than other reptiles.

They also had curvy necks, so they could move their heads better than other reptiles. However, they still weren't the top hunters!

### Old fish

The coelacanth (SEE-la-canth) appeared in Triassic pools and rivers 380 million years ago. Amazingly, this tough group of fish is still alive today! They live in the Indian Ocean.

## The top hunter

The hunter Herrerasaurus, one of the largest early dinosaurs, was as long as a family car. But it was only half the length of reptiles like Saurosuchus that were around at the time!

# Dino world

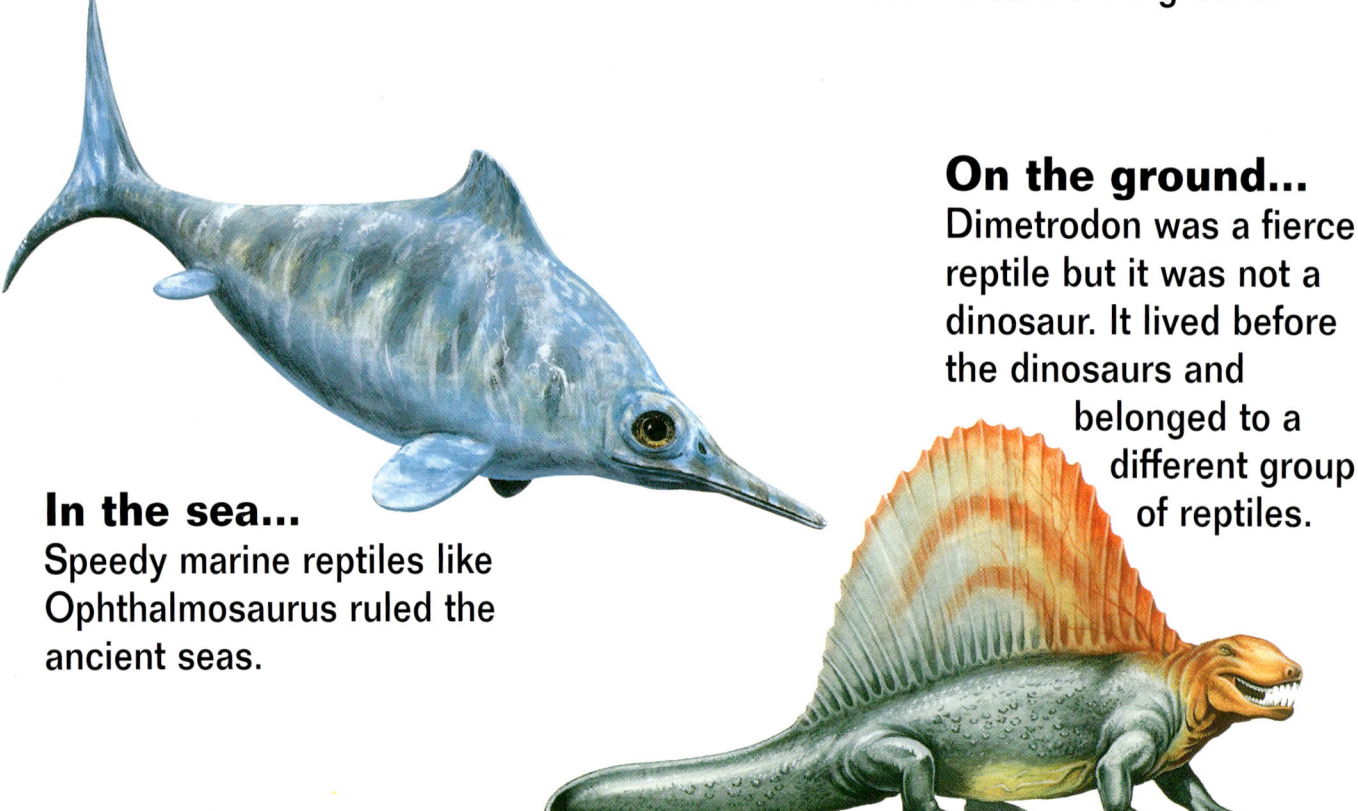

## What else lived then?
When dinosaurs appeared on Earth, there were already many other animals around. The dinosaurs were just one group of land-living reptiles. Other reptiles took to the seas and skies.

## In the air...
Pterosaurs, like Cearadactylus, were reptiles that flew rather than lived on the ground.

## On the ground...
Dimetrodon was a fierce reptile but it was not a dinosaur. It lived before the dinosaurs and belonged to a different group of reptiles.

## In the sea...
Speedy marine reptiles like Ophthalmosaurus ruled the ancient seas.

# The family tree

## Dino cousins

The dinosaurs were just one group of reptiles. But some looked alike and some looked very different, so how did they divide up?

This family tree shows you how. You can see which types were most closely related.

## Dinosauria

(di-no-SORE-ee-ah)
The group of animals called Dinosauria contains all of the dinosaurs that ever lived. The Dinosauria group is divided into two smaller groups or 'orders', called Saurischia and Ornithischia.

## Saurischia

(SORE-isk-EE-ah)
Saurischia means 'reptile-hipped' in Latin. Dinosaurs in this order had hip bones that looked like those of today's reptiles. The order is divided into two suborders, Theropoda and Sauropodomorpha.

## Ornithischia

(ORN-ith-isk-EE-ah)
Ornithischia means 'bird-hipped' in Latin. These dinosaurs' hips were the same shape as today's birds.

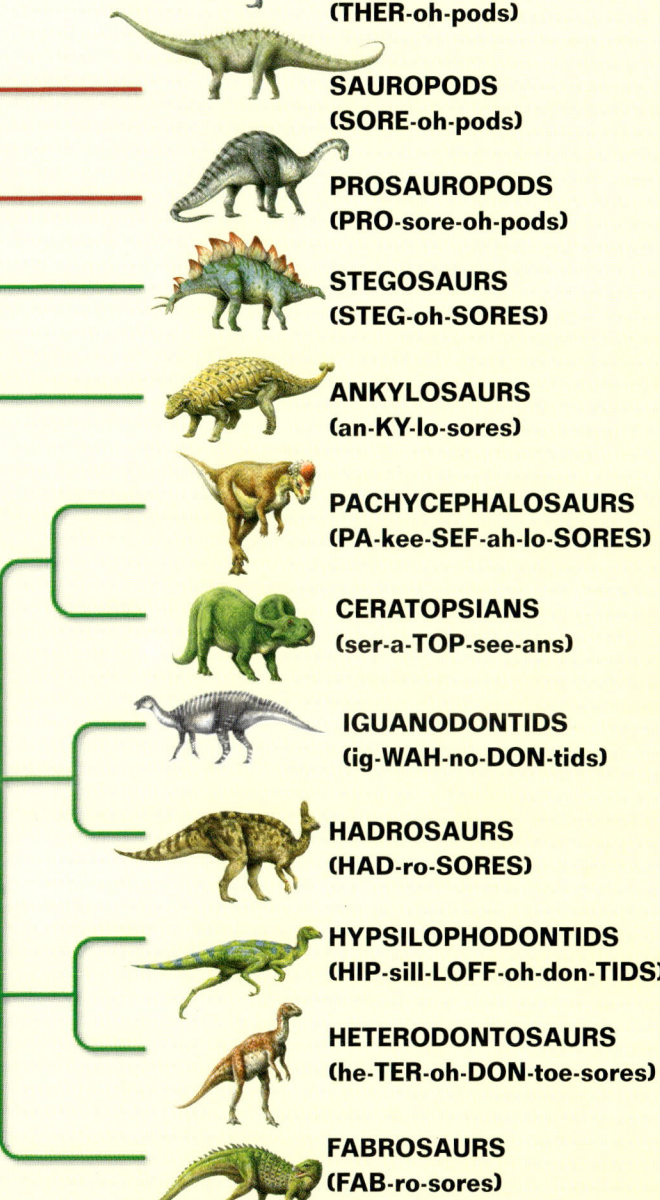

**THEROPODS**
(THER-oh-pods)

**SAUROPODS**
(SORE-oh-pods)

**PROSAUROPODS**
(PRO-sore-oh-pods)

**STEGOSAURS**
(STEG-oh-SORES)

**ANKYLOSAURS**
(an-KY-lo-sores)

**PACHYCEPHALOSAURS**
(PA-kee-SEF-ah-lo-SORES)

**CERATOPSIANS**
(ser-a-TOP-see-ans)

**IGUANODONTIDS**
(ig-WAH-no-DON-tids)

**HADROSAURS**
(HAD-ro-SORES)

**HYPSILOPHODONTIDS**
(HIP-sill-LOFF-oh-don-TIDS)

**HETERODONTOSAURS**
(he-TER-oh-DON-toe-sores)

**FABROSAURS**
(FAB-ro-sores)

# Theropods

## Theropods
(THER-oh-pods)
Theropods were meat-eating dinosaurs.
Dinosaur experts believe that some
theropods ate plants too.

## Dino-bird
When you look at the feet
of an emu it is easy to
see why some scientists
think birds are descended
from dinosaurs.

## Tyrannosaurus rex
The fierce hunter, T. rex, was a
theropod. It was heavier and
stronger than a bull elephant
and had dagger-like teeth.

# Sauropods

## Sauropods
(SORE-oh-pods)
These were the biggest
land animals ever! They
were huge plant-eaters
with long necks to reach
the treetops and long
tails for balance.

## Diplodocus
With its whiplash tail and
clawed feet, this ten-tonne
plant-eater could look
after itself!

### Crushing feet
Diplodocus' feet were
almost identical to those
of a modern elephant.

13

# Prosauropods

## Prosauropods
(PRO-sore-oh-pods)
Like the huge sauropods, these plant-eaters had long necks and tails, but were smaller than sauropods, making them an easier target for hunters.

## Plateosaurus
This hefty eating-machine had a strong jaw to help it browse on tough plants.

# Stegosaurs

## Stegosaurs
(STEG-oh-SORES)
These large plant-eaters are famous for the plates
on their backs and their lethal tail-spikes.

## Stegosaurus
It was fearsome-looking and
huge, but the brain of this
weighty giant was walnut-sized!

# Ankylosaurs

## Ankylosaurs
(an-KYE-low-sores)
These were the armoured plant-eaters. Some had tail-clubs and spikes which they could use to fend off attacking meat-eaters.

## Ankylosaurus
This dino would stand and fight, well protected by its bone-tipped tail.

# Pachycephalosaurs

## Pachycephalosaurs
(PA-kee-SEF-a-low-SORES)
These plant-eaters had tough,
thickened skulls and walked on two legs.

## Pachycephalosaurus
With its thick skullcap, this
dinosaur could have given
rivals a violent head-butt to
defend itself.

# Ceratopsians

## Ceratopsians
(ser-a-TOP-see-ans)
Most of these heavy, plant-eating dinosaurs had horns and neck frills.

## Protoceratops
This dinosaur had a horny beak to cut through tough plant stems.

# Iguanodontids

**Iguanodontids**
(ig-WAH-no-don-tids)
These large plant-eaters walked on all fours but could run fast, when attacked, by rising up on to their back legs.

**Iguanodon**
This famous plant-eater was the second dinosaur fossil ever found.

19

# Hadrosaurs

**Hadrosaurs**
(HAD-ro-SORES)
Sometimes called 'duck-billed'
dinosaurs, these dinosaurs had flat,
beak-like jaws.

**Corythosaurus**
The strange crest on this
dinosaur's head was
probably used to make
sounds to its herd.

# Hypsilophodontids

## Hypsilophodontids
(hip-si-LOAF-o-don-tids)
Most were small and moved
quickly on two legs but some
were larger, four-legged creatures.

## Hypsilophodon
This speedy plant-eater was
just a bit taller than you!

# Heterodontosaurs

**Heterodontosaurs**
(HET-er-oh-DONT-o-sores)
These were all small,
two-legged plant-eaters.

**Heterodontosaurus**
This nippy dinosaur had
dog-like teeth, even
though it ate plants.

# Fabrosaurs

**Fabrosaurs**
(FAB-ro-sores)
These were the smallest
dinosaurs. Some were no
bigger than a chicken!

**Scutellosaurus**
Its armoured back and body
protected this dinosaur if it
was attacked as it ate.

# How fossils are made

### What is a fossil?

Fossils are the remains of living things preserved in rock. When animals die, their bodies are usually eaten or they rot away into the soil. But sometimes a process called "fossilization" takes place which can preserve a living thing for all time. Fossilization needs lots of things to happen.

There were many ways that a dinosaur could have become a fossil.

### 1 Death of a dinosaur

Imagine that a large plant-eating dinosaur called Apatosaurus has died. Perhaps it gets washed into a nearby river.

### 2 Rotting body

As it rots, it fills with gas and floats along the river. Its soft parts, like its stomach, carry on rotting and making gas.

### 3 The body bag bursts!

Finally, the body is so full of gas that it bursts – or perhaps a crocodile takes a bite and it pops! The body sinks to the soft mud at the bottom of the river.

### 4 Buried in mud

On the river bed, the soft tissues rot away. The remaining bones get covered in fine sand. Layers of sand build up and bury it.

### 5 Millions of years later...

The layers of sand have been pressed into rock, trapping the bones inside. Salts and other minerals seep into the bones. Slowly the bones harden and also turn to rock – but rock with a different colour and texture. The Apatosaurus skeleton is now a fossil.

# Rebuilding a dinosaur

## Putting the skeleton back together

Dinosaur experts look at living animals to help them rebuild fossilized dinosaurs' skeletons. Certain clues on this Coelophysis skeleton help the experts to work out how it lived.

Holes in the skull made it light so this dinosaur could move its head quickly.

This bone, the ilium, connected the hips to the spine.

No ribs in the back half of the body mean it was light and could run fast.

The ribs protected the soft organs, like the heart and liver.

The pubis held the muscles that pulled the legs forwards.

## Look closer

This Coelophysis fossil has a baby Coelophysis inside it. It looks as if this dinosaur was a cannibal!

**The spine was made up of bones called "vertebrae".**

**The ischium held the muscles that pulled the legs backwards.**

# Life in dinoland

## A common sight
Hypsilophodon was one of the
most common dinosaurs, living in
most places in the world for over
**100 million years.**

## Monkey puzzles
These trees were around
when dinosaurs walked the
Earth and we can still see
them today. They grow wild
in South America and are
planted in gardens in many
other countries.

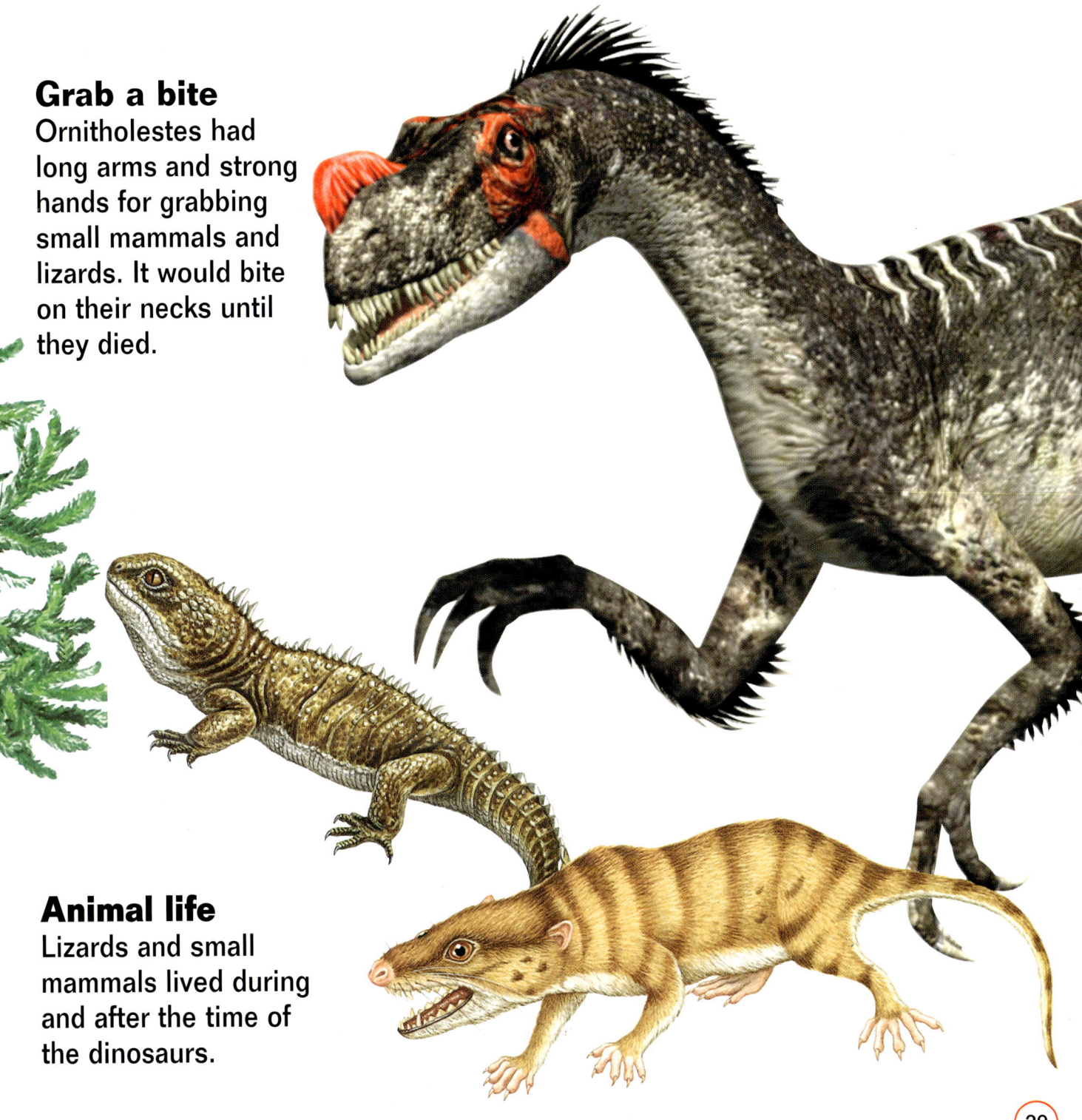

## Grab a bite

Ornitholestes had long arms and strong hands for grabbing small mammals and lizards. It would bite on their necks until they died.

## Animal life

Lizards and small mammals lived during and after the time of the dinosaurs.

# Dinosaur eggs

## How do we know?

We know that dinosaurs laid eggs because nests of fossil eggs have been found.

Some mothers, like this Maiasaura, stayed by the eggs to care for the young, but some left the eggs to hatch on their own.

**Buried in sand**
Giant sauropods such as Titanosaurus laid round, football-sized eggs in trenches, then buried them.

## Egg-laying

Some dinosaurs made nests in which to hatch their eggs. Because dinosaurs were so big, they often laid their eggs in special patterns to avoid crushing them.

**Spirals**
Troodon nests have been found with the eggs laid in neat spirals.

# Baby care

## Safe in the nest

This is a model of a fossil Maiasaura nest. The eggshells inside had been crushed, showing that the babies stayed in the nest for some time after they were born.

## Feed me!

These babies had weak ankles and couldn't walk. The mother would have fed them.

# From babies to adults

## Break for freedom
A baby Protoceratops hatches from its egg. It would have had large eyes and a big head in comparison to its body.

## Growing pains
A young Protoceratops' body grew faster than its head so that when it was fully grown, its head was the right size for its body.

## Adults keep growing
Adult dinosaurs carried on growing throughout their lives, although at a slower rate than their young. Turtles today grow in the same way.

## Up and away

To fly, adult Rhamphorhynchus
needed much larger wings in
proportion to their bodies than
youngsters did. So its wings
grew faster than its body.

# Dinosaur senses

## Living clues

Many scientists believe that birds are descended from dinosaurs. Looking at birds helps us to understand how dinosaurs may have used their senses.

For example, owls hear so well that they can target their prey by listening to the tiny sounds they make. It's possible that dinosaurs did too!

## Sight

Leaellynasaura had huge eyes so that it could see during the dark winters of the Antarctic.

## Sharp-eyed eagles

Some birds have amazingly good eyesight. Sharp-eyed eagles can spot small animals even when they are flying hundreds of metres above them.

## Smell

Meat-eaters had a good sense of smell. In fact, the space for T. rex's smell sensors in its skull were larger than its brain cavity! So it was more important for T. rex to smell than to think!

## Hearing

Fossils of dinosaurs' fine ear bones are hard to find but other signs show that hearing was a key sense.

Saurolophus had a nose bag and 'talked' to the herd by inflating it.

# Dinosaurs' diets

## What's for dinner?

Dinosaurs were either meat-eaters or plant-eaters, just as animals are today. A dinosaur's body and jaws were specially designed to help it find and eat its food.

## Meat-eating dinosaurs

T. rex (below) was the king of these killers. They all had sharp teeth for ripping into their prey and strong jaws for pulling off chunks of meat.

## Plant-eaters

Tough plants posed no problem for plant-eaters like Diplodocus (above). Many had stones called 'gastroliths' in their stomachs to help grind up the food.

## Special equipment

Hypsilophodontids, like Tenontosaurus (above), had horny beaks. They used this beak to snip off leaves then used grinding teeth at the back of their mouths to chew them up.

# Teeth and beaks

### Chewy-saurus
Camptosaurus was the first large dinosaur to chew its food. This meant that it could absorb more goodness from tough plants than other plant-eaters could, and so could survive dry seasons when food was scarce.

## Replacement beak

Edmontosaurus had no front teeth to bite the plants it ate. Instead, its upper and lower jaws were covered by a tough, sharp beak. Like fingernails, this grew from the skin and constantly renewed itself. This meant Edmontosaurus could eat tough, woody plant matter without losing or blunting its beak.

# Hunters!

## Catching dinner

There were many fearsome meat-eating dinosaurs. Those that hunted – the predators – were the most deadly and dangerous. Each developed clever hunting methods to catch their prey.

## Lethal talons

Deinonychus used its massive toe claw to slash at its prey.

## Team work

By hunting in packs, Deinonychus could attack and kill the much bigger Tenontosaurus. They leapt onto its back and sides and clawed it until it weakened. But some might also have been wounded by the plant-eater's whip-like tail.

## Lone killers

Coelophysis probably hunted alone, speeding after small animals. Its skin may have had a camouflage pattern to help it to ambush its prey

### Fish hunter

Not all meat-eating dinosaurs hunted other dinosaurs. Some small meat-eaters hunted lizards and mammals. Others, like Baryonyx (below), ate fish! Scientists know this because it had long jaws like those of today's fish-eating crocodiles.

# Dinosaur battles

## Why fight?

Dinosaurs fought for all sorts of reasons. Some fought for territory when there wasn't enough food to go round. In the mating season, males would battle for mates. Meat-eaters often fought over a kill. Sometimes a meat-eater would attack a plant-eater, and the plant-eater would fight back.

## Survival

With their thick armour and razor-like teeth and claws, dinosaur battles were deadly and dangerous. Below, the meat-eater Ceratosaurus may have bitten off more than he can chew in trying to kill Stegosaurus.

## For mates

Some male dinosaurs fought to win mates, and different dinosaurs fought in different ways. Horned plant-eaters, such as Triceratops, battled head-to-head. The weaker dinosaur would lose the battle and the mate, so only the fittest survived.

# The King!

## Killing bite

Tyrannosaurus rex was a giant biting machine. Its huge skull was equipped with strong muscles to power its jaws and it had the biggest teeth of any meat-eating land animal.

**BITE-POWER**
T. rex had huge neck bones lined with strong muscles for added bite-power!

**DEATH GRIP**
T. rex grabbed small animals and shook them to death.

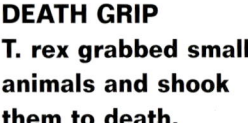

## Charge!

Scientists think that T. rex attacked like a shark, charging in with its mouth open. Death was quick as its five-tonne body smashed into its victim.

**TINY HANDS**
T. rex had tiny arms and hands for such a big dinosaur. Even so, its arms were three times as strong as a man's.

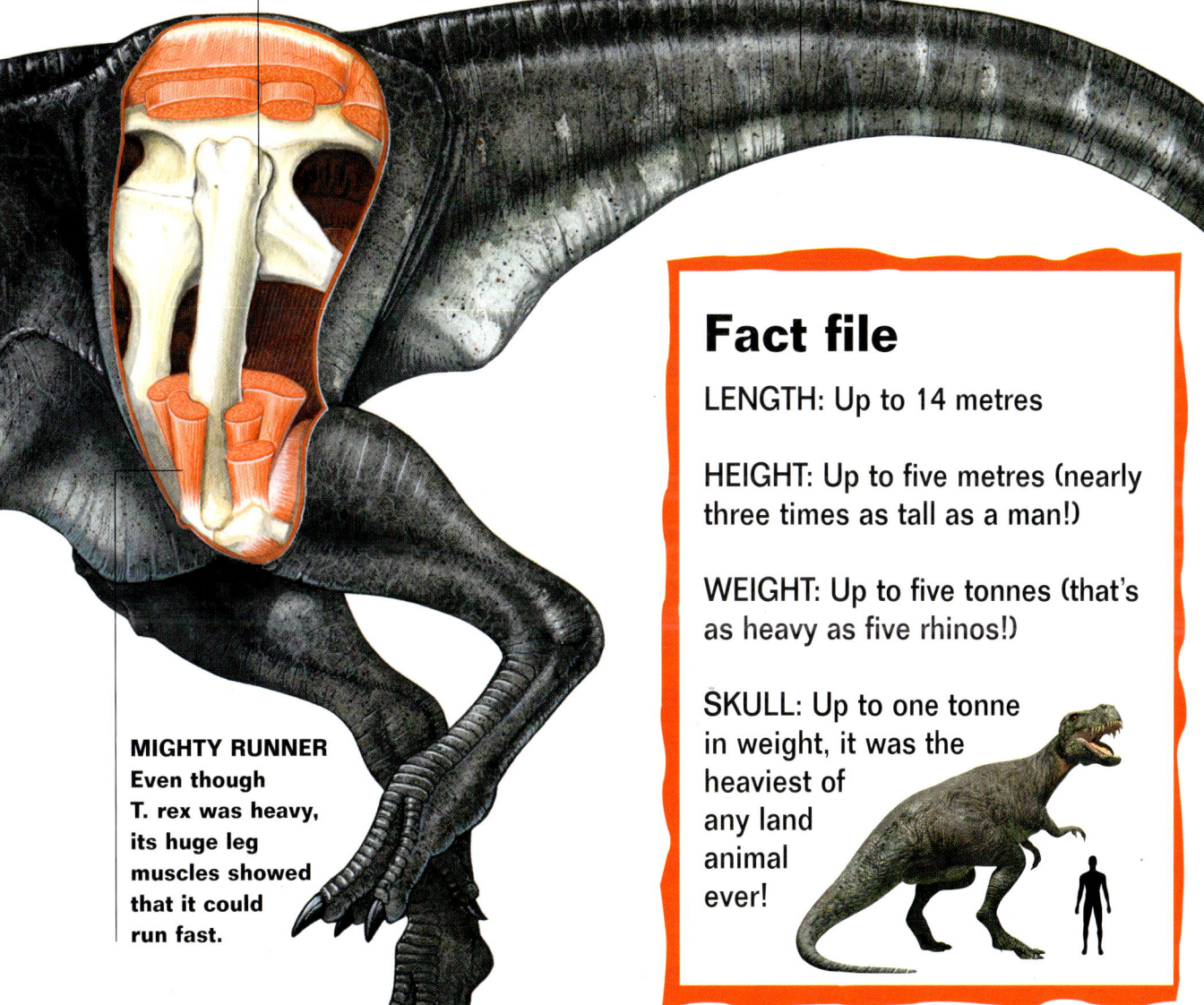

**CENTRE POINT**
The massive hip bones were the point around which the rest of T. rex's body moved. They linked the leg bones to the spine.

**WELL-BALANCED**
T. rex held its tail out when it was running to balance the weight of its huge head.

**MIGHTY RUNNER**
Even though T. rex was heavy, its huge leg muscles showed that it could run fast.

# Fact file

LENGTH: Up to 14 metres

HEIGHT: Up to five metres (nearly three times as tall as a man!)

WEIGHT: Up to five tonnes (that's as heavy as five rhinos!)

SKULL: Up to one tonne in weight, it was the heaviest of any land animal ever!

# Slow but sure

## Plodding plant-eaters

Plant-eaters needed to protect themselves from predators, either by running away if they were agile or having body armour if they were big and slow.

The plant-eating Stegosaurus was like a dinosaur tank. It was built to survive attack.

## Fact file

LENGTH: Up to 13 metres. That's as long as a train carriage!

HEIGHT: Seven metres – as high as a house!

WEIGHT: Seven tonnes – the same weight as 100 men!

PLATES: Stegosaurus' largest plate was as big as a kitchen table!

**SAVING ITS NECK**
The skin under the neck was studded with tiny bones. This protected its windpipe from a meat-eater's suffocating bite.

**BIG BLADE**
Stegosaurus' front legs were packed with muscles to support its weight. These were joined to its shoulder.

**SKIN AND BONE**
The bony plates were
covered with skin.
They were not joined
to any other bones,
but swayed as the
dinosaur moved.

# Armoured tanks

## Self-defence

Many plant-eating dinosaurs were so heavy and slow-moving that they were forced to stand and defend themselves against predators. They were not able to run away – but they could fight back!

## Indestructible!

Ankylosaurus was virtually untouchable. Its entire body was coated in bony studs. If it was attacked, it just squatted down, presenting its attacker with a bony shield. But its swinging tail club could deliver a bone-crushing blow.

## Armour

Armour is a great way for slow animals to protect themselves. Many creatures that would otherwise be easy targets for meat-eaters are left alone because of their armour. The hedgehog and woodlouse are two examples. Hardly any creatures bother these well-protected animals.

## Spiky armour

Tarchia was much more spiky than Ankylosaurus. It lived in Mongolia 65 million years ago.

# Spiked defence

## Tough Triceratops

Triceratops was a plant-eater but it wasn't unarmed. The two horns on its brow were almost a metre long and could pierce the tough hide of an attacker, causing serious injury or even death.

## Big head

Torosaurus had a three-
metre-long skull, the largest
of any land animal ever. The male
used his frill to attract a mate and
his huge horns to fend off hunters.

# Strange weapons

## Iguanodon

It may have been a plant-eater, but Iguanodon was no wimp! If attacked, it used its thumb spike to stab its attacker.

## Dacentrurus

Any meat-eater would think twice about chomping down on these spikes, but Dacentrurus could also rear up on its hind legs like bears do today, and bring its two-tonne body down on an enemy.

# Dinosaur speed!

## The need for speed
The meat-eating hunters had to be swift on their feet as they needed speed to catch their prey.

## Born to run
Deinonychus was built for speed. It weighed the same as today's fastest animal, the cheetah, and could run just as fast to catch prey.

## Struthiomimus
Does this creature look familiar? Its name means 'ostrich mimic' and it could run even faster than a modern ostrich!

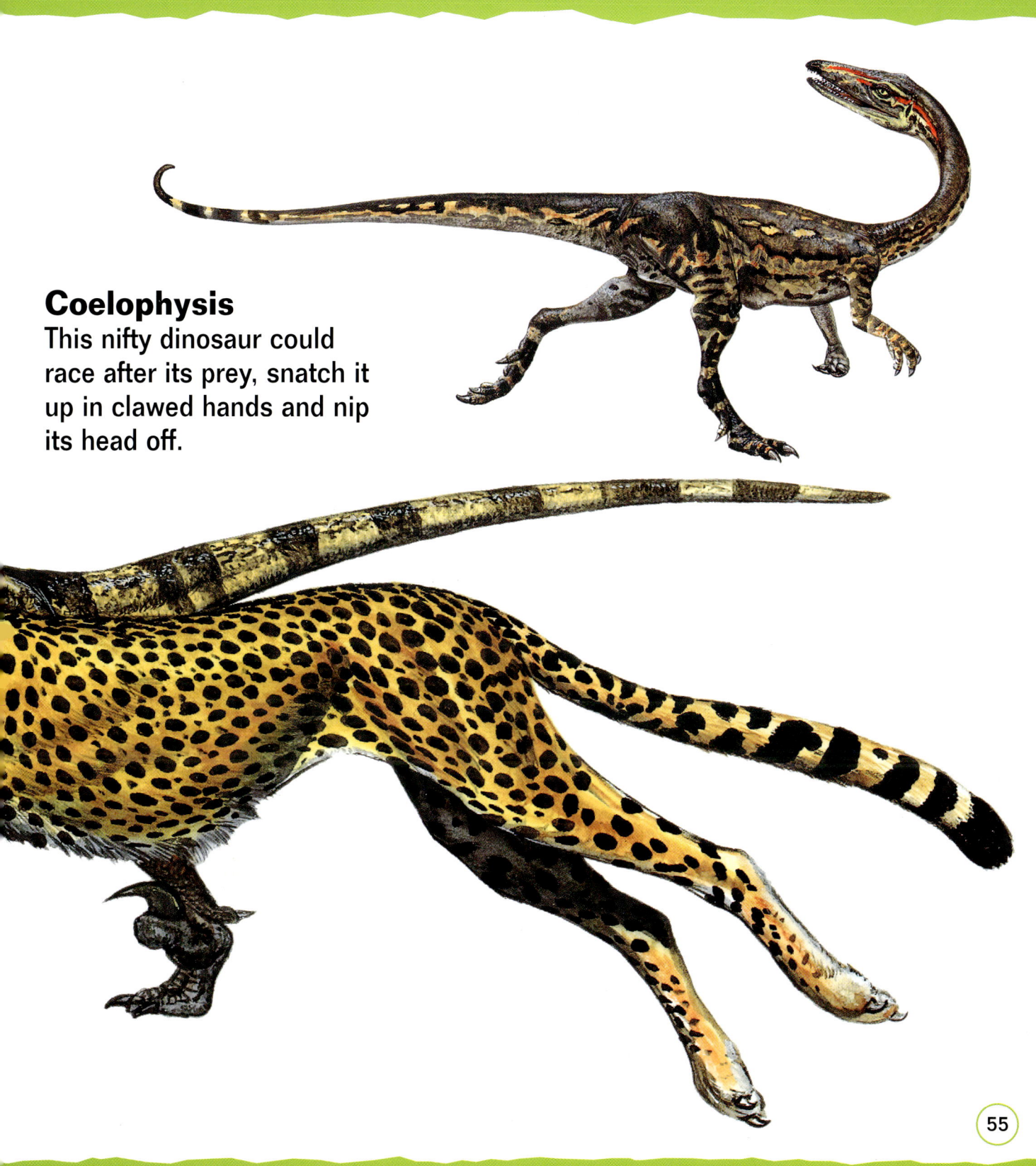

## Coelophysis

This nifty dinosaur could race after its prey, snatch it up in clawed hands and nip its head off.

# Ultimate killer

## Clever hunter

Utahraptor's killing skills were unbeatable. As well as vicious claws, it had a large brain and could work with other Utahraptor to hunt down and kill larger plant-eaters.

## Fact file

LENGTH: Up to six metres. That's as long as a Transit van!

HEIGHT: Up to two metres – not much taller than a man.

WEIGHT: Utahraptor weighed about half a tonne.

TOE CLAW: Its 20 centimetre-long claw could slash the toughest hide.

**TEETH**
Utahraptor had 60 teeth. Its teeth were curved backwards and serrated to slice through flesh.

**HANDS**
Each hand had three hook-like claws. Utahraptor used them to grasp moving prey.

**SKIN**
Utahraptor may have been camouflaged so it could creep up on its victims unseen.

**TAIL BONES**
The bones in the last three quarters of the tail were joined together by bony rods and muscles. This made the tail stiff.

**TAIL**
The long tail could be flicked from left to right, helping it to twist and turn after its prey.

## Flexi-claw!
The killing claw was very flexible. Utahraptor could easily move it up and down. It could be flicked backward and forward to slash again and again.

**LEGS**
Utahraptor's slender legs were built for sprinting. Its bones were hollow, making them light but strong.

**FEET**
Utahraptor used its feet to grip the ground as it ran and to wound and kill its prey.

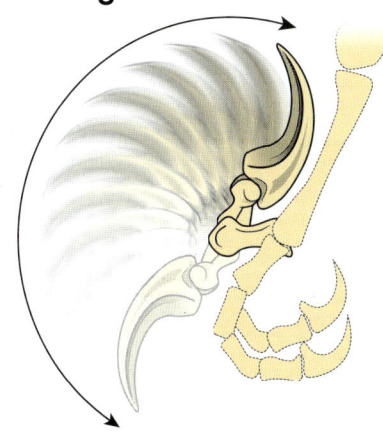

# The deadliest

## Monster mouth

Allosaurus was built to kill. This monster was better armed than almost any other dinosaur.

With grappling claws and a mouth full of fiercely sharp, stabbing teeth, Allosaurus could tackle all but the most massive plant-eaters.

**HOLE IN THE HEAD**
The skull had large gaps in it to make it lighter. This helped Allosaurus to move its head more quickly when attacking.

## Fact file

LENGTH: Up to 12 metres.

HEIGHT: 4.5 metres – taller than a double-decker!

WEIGHT: Around three tonnes.

JAWS: Allosaurus' jaws were hinged right at the back. This gave it a bite that was more than a metre long!

**CRUSHING BITE**
The muscles that pulled the jaws together were massive, giving Allosaurus an incredibly powerful bite.

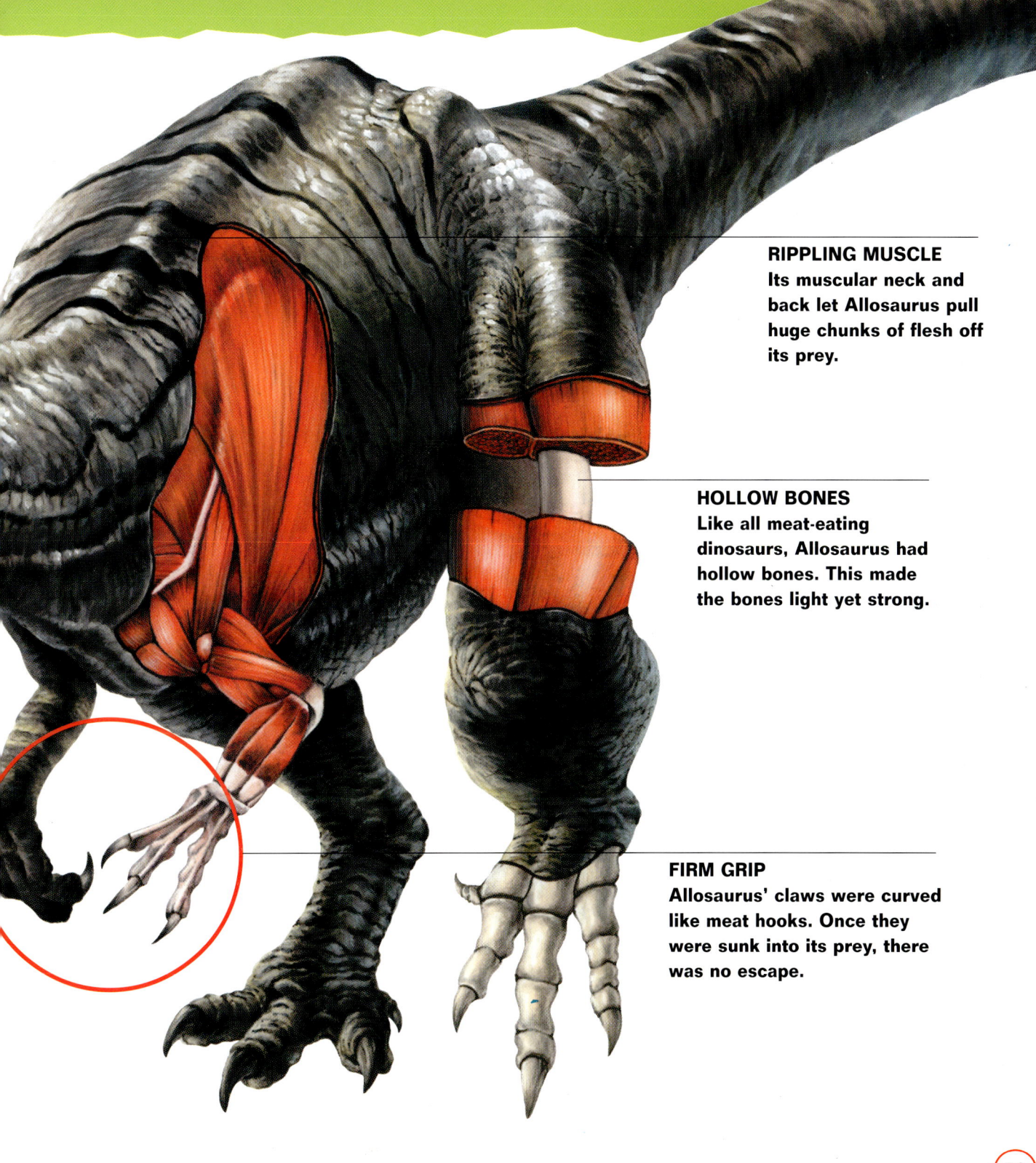

**RIPPLING MUSCLE**
Its muscular neck and back let Allosaurus pull huge chunks of flesh off its prey.

**HOLLOW BONES**
Like all meat-eating dinosaurs, Allosaurus had hollow bones. This made the bones light yet strong.

**FIRM GRIP**
Allosaurus' claws were curved like meat hooks. Once they were sunk into its prey, there was no escape.

# The greediest!

## Greedy guts!

Diplodocus was one of the greediest animals ever! This dinosaur was so big, and there was so little goodness in its food, that it had to eat almost all the time to stay alive.

**LONG NECK**
The neck was ten metres long! It was made up of 15 bones which were huge at the base and got smaller towards the head.

## Fact file

LENGTH: 30 metres – the same as three lorries parked end to end!

HEIGHT: Five metres at the hip – that's as tall as a giraffe!

WEIGHT: Eleven tonnes – that's heavier than two African elephants!

TAIL: Its tail made up almost half of its length. It contained more than 70 bones.

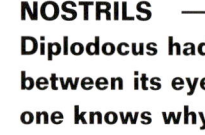

**NOSTRILS**
Diplodocus had nostrils between its eyes! No one knows why. Some experts think that it had a trunk like an elephant.

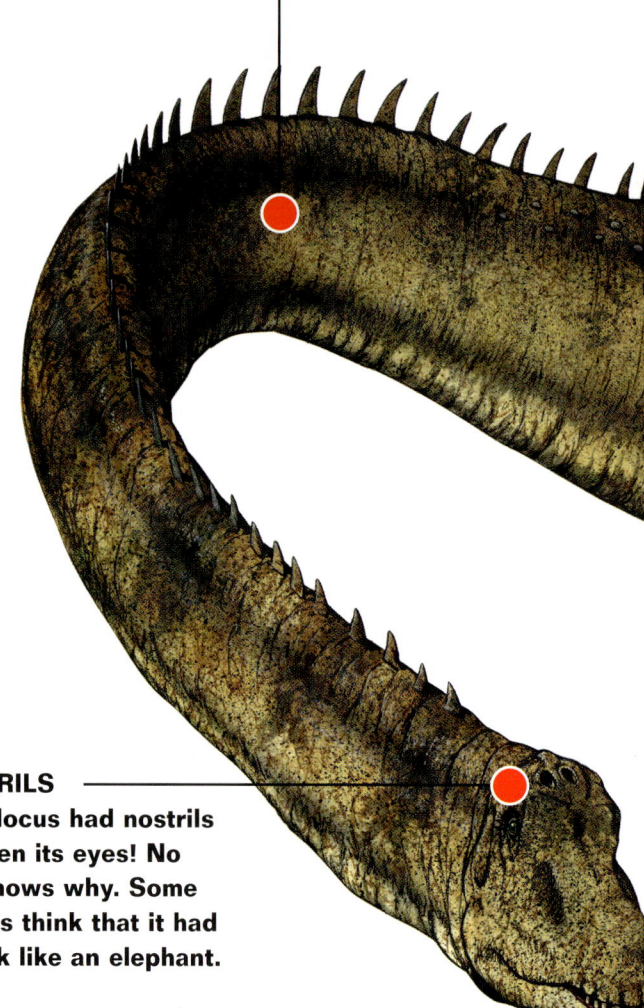

**TWIN TOWERS**
Two spines stuck up from each back bone. These held up rope-like ligaments which lifted the neck and tail.

**GRINDING GIZZARD**
Diplodocus swallowed pebbles which were used in the gizzard to mash up the tough leaves that it ate.

**THE TAIL**
Diplodocus cracked its tail like a whip to keep in touch with herd members and fend off meat-eaters.

**LEATHERY SPINES**
Fossils show that Diplodocus had a row of leathery spines along its back like an iguana does today. These may have been for display.

**CLAWS**
Some of the nails on the feet were pointed like claws.

# The smallest

### Little lizards

We often think of dinosaurs as giants but they came in all shapes and sizes. Some were tiny and hunted smaller creatures.

### Cretaceous chicken

Microvenator (MY-crow-ve-NAY-tor) was little bigger than a chicken, making it one of the smallest dinosaurs of the Early Cretaceous.

# Giant guts

## Hard grind

Seismosaurus did not have chewing teeth. Instead, it swallowed stones, called "gastroliths", to grind up tough plants, just as birds swallow grit to break up seeds.

A Seismosaurus fossil has been found containing 230 stones!

## Long neck

An amazing 45 metres from head to tail, Seismosaurus was the longest dinosaur ever.

# The biggest

## Big, bigger, biggest!

New dinosaurs are being dug up all the time. Some are enormous, but that's not to say that fossil hunters have found the biggest ever… yet!

## Towering giant

The tallest and heaviest dinosaur ever found was Ultrasaurus. It was 18 metres tall – higher than a three-storey building.

## A heavy matter

Brachiosaurus was one of the heaviest dinosaurs, weighing 70 tonnes, which is fourteen times heavier than an elephant.

# The fastest

## Zippy Zephyro

The tiny dinosaur Zephyrosaurus was one of the fastest. It was the size of an Alsatian dog and ran on two legs.

## Quick escape

For some plant-eating dinosaurs, speed was the only way to escape fierce, hungry hunters.

Othnielia was the expert. It was too small for big meat-eaters to bother with and too fast for other hunters to catch!

# Strange but true

## Duckbilled dinosaurs

Dinosaurs came in all sorts of shapes and their strange body parts had special uses. This Anatotitan used its beak to rake up lots of plants in one mouthful.

## Thick head

Pachycephalosaurus' domed head was 25 centimetres thick. It was used to butt other males when it was fighting for a mate.

# Dino lookalikes

## Just like an ostrich

Ostriches are the fastest flightless birds alive today. Some dinosaurs, such as Dromiceiomimus, Struthiomimus and Gallimimus (from left to right), looked like ostriches and they may have moved even faster.

## Walking on water

The basilisk is a lizard that moves so fast that it can run on water. Coelophysis would have run in the same way.

**Birds of a feather**
One of the most exciting fossil finds ever was Archaeopteryx, a bird that lived 150 million years ago. Archaeopteryx is still the oldest creature with feathered wings known to man. It makes a crucial link between dinosaurs and birds. Men working on a German fossil bed in 1861 found the ancient bird's remains, complete with feathers!

# Sea monster

## Reptiles of the deep

Liopleurodon was a sea reptile and one of the most deadly hunters the seas have ever seen.

It had a super-sharp sense of smell which helped it to track its prey. And when it found a victim, it attacked with explosive speed.

**BIG BITE**
Liopleurodon's jaws were vast. This monster could have eaten most other sea reptiles in a single gulp.

## Fact file

LENGTH: Up to 25 metres. That's as long as a swimming pool!

WEIGHT: Up to 150 tonnes! That's the same weight as 30 T. rex put together!

FLIPPERS: Each flipper was over three metres long. You could have hidden a small car under each one!

**SPIKY TEETH**
Liopleurodon's teeth stuck out. This made its mouth even longer so it could grab at victims that tried to dodge out of the way.

**FLEXI-NECK**
Liopleurodon's flexible neck allowed it to twist its head to catch even fast-moving creatures.

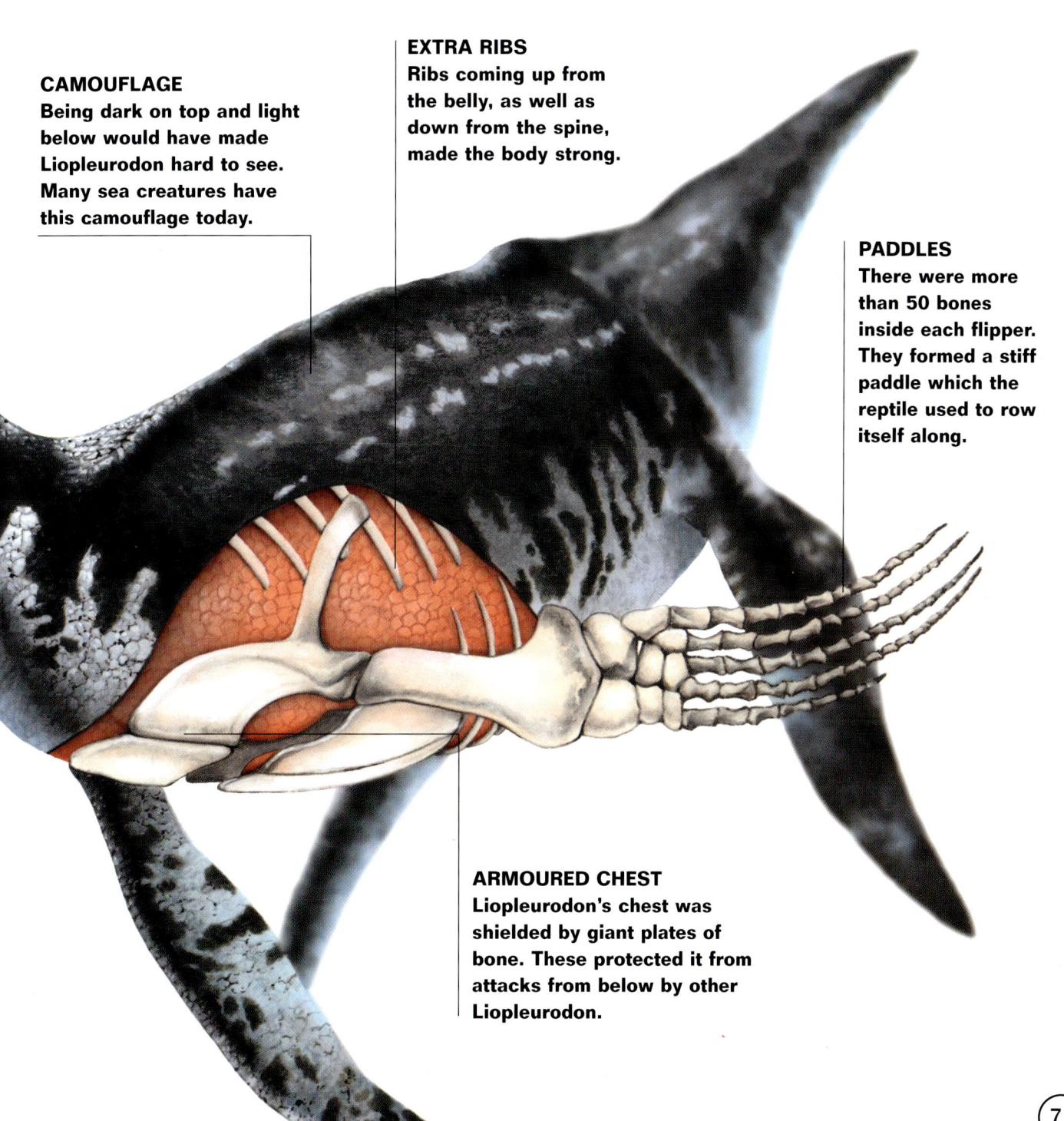

**CAMOUFLAGE**
Being dark on top and light below would have made Liopleurodon hard to see. Many sea creatures have this camouflage today.

**EXTRA RIBS**
Ribs coming up from the belly, as well as down from the spine, made the body strong.

**PADDLES**
There were more than 50 bones inside each flipper. They formed a stiff paddle which the reptile used to row itself along.

**ARMOURED CHEST**
Liopleurodon's chest was shielded by giant plates of bone. These protected it from attacks from below by other Liopleurodon.

# Pterosaurs

## Winged reptiles

Dinosaurs were land animals and could not fly. Flying reptiles were called 'pterosaurs'. They had large flaps of skin which formed wings. Some ate insects but larger ones ate fish or carrion.

Ornithocheirus was a huge pterosaur. Let's find out how it flew.

**WINGS**
Ornithocheirus' wings covered an area of 12 square metres. That's the same as eight duvets!

## Fact file

LENGTH: Three and a half metres. The same as three six-year-olds holding hands with their arms stretched out.

WEIGHT: Up to 100 kilogrammes – a bit heavier than a fully-grown man.

WINGSPAN: Up to 12 metres -- more than most modern light aircraft!

FINGERS: The finger that held each wing out was three metres long! But it was made up of just four bones – one more bone than our own fingers!

## Giant of the skies

The family of pterosaurs called 'Euthygnatha' included the biggest flying reptile of all, Quetzalcoatlus (above), which had a 14-metre wingspan!

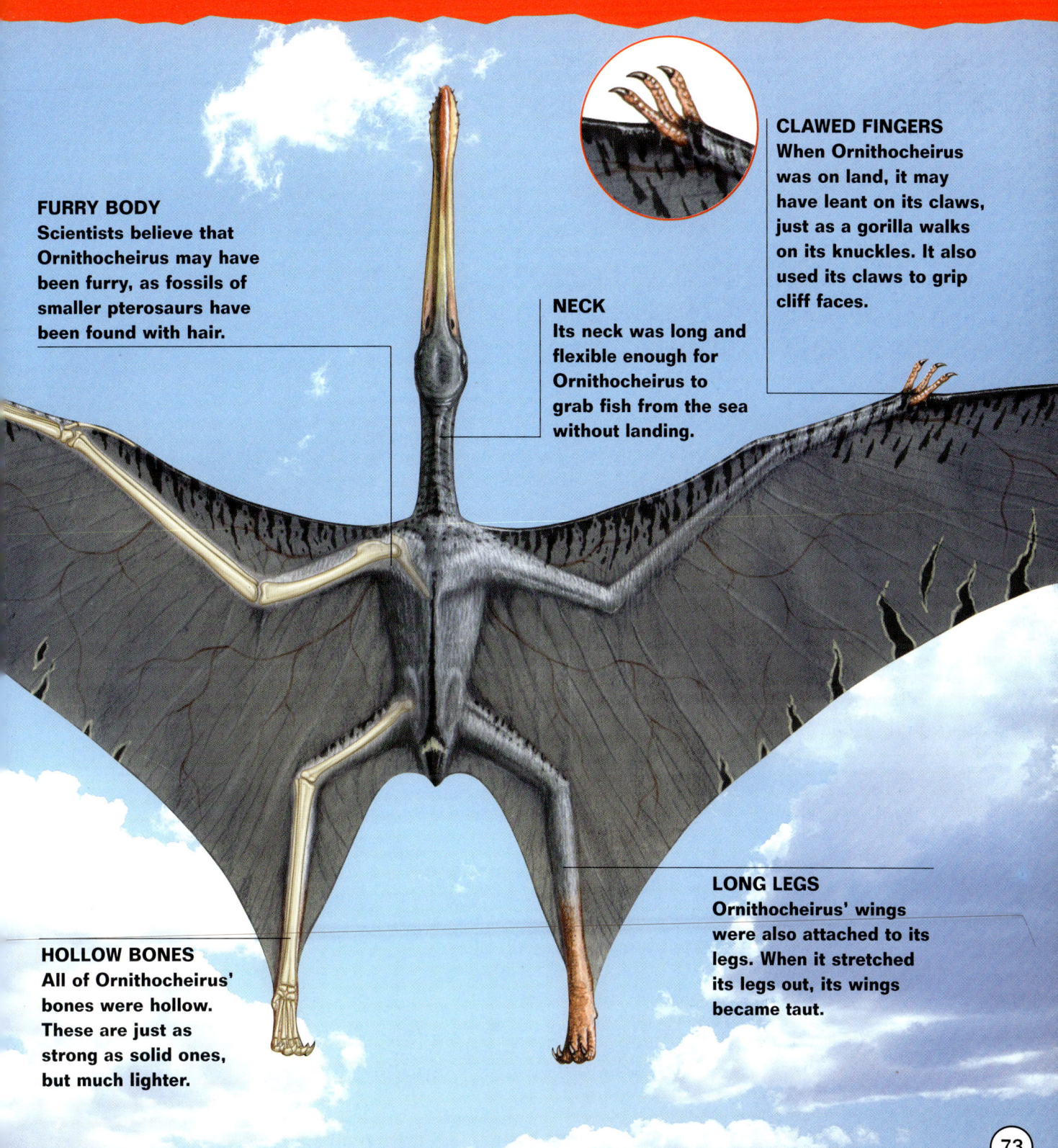

**FURRY BODY**
Scientists believe that Ornithocheirus may have been furry, as fossils of smaller pterosaurs have been found with hair.

**CLAWED FINGERS**
When Ornithocheirus was on land, it may have leant on its claws, just as a gorilla walks on its knuckles. It also used its claws to grip cliff faces.

**NECK**
Its neck was long and flexible enough for Ornithocheirus to grab fish from the sea without landing.

**LONG LEGS**
Ornithocheirus' wings were also attached to its legs. When it stretched its legs out, its wings became taut.

**HOLLOW BONES**
All of Ornithocheirus' bones were hollow. These are just as strong as solid ones, but much lighter.

# The end of the dinosaurs

## What happened to the dinos?

No one knows. Scientists think that dust clouds, caused by a meteorite strike and volcanic action, blocked the sunlight. Earth became cold and dark.

As the plants died, plant-eating dinosaurs starved. Then meat-eaters died of hunger and cold too.

## Prove it!

Scientists have found a vast buried crater in Mexico. Samples from the crater contain a metal which is rare on Earth but often found in meteorites, called 'iridium'.

## Deathly darkness

The dust made by a meteorite impact would have caused the skies to darken for months, killing off the vegetation that plant-eating dinosaurs ate.

## Volcanoes

Iridium, the metal found in meteorites, is also found in volcanic dust. In India, lava beds which date back to the Late Cretaceous have iridium in them. So volcanic action could have added to the dust clouds.

## Changing sea levels

Another theory was that temperatures changed when sea levels dropped at the end of the Late Cretaceous. As small seas drained away, the weather became more extreme, killing many types of plants and animals.

# How mammals survived

### Death blast

About 65 million years ago, the Earth was hit by a huge meteorite. The dust cloud rising from this blocked the sun, and the Earth cooled down. The dinosaurs died, but many mammals survived and are still successful today.

Didelphodon

Ctenacodon

Morganucodon

### The first mammals

Mammals appeared 220 million years ago, 10 million years after the dinosaurs arrived. They were tiny insect-eaters, like Morganucodon.

Mammals hardly changed while the dinosaurs were around. A few, like Ctenacodon, began living in trees and some, like Didelphodon, grew bigger.

## Why did they survive?

Mammals survived the harsh conditions on Earth that killed the dinosaurs because they were smaller and more adaptable than dinosaurs.

These animals ate insects and made burrows which may have helped them survive extinction.

## Mammals today – like us!

Today there are three kinds of mammal. Most, like dolphins and humans, give birth to well-developed, live young.

Marsupials, such as kangaroos, give birth to tiny babies, which they carry in a pouch.

The monotremes, like the duck-billed platypus, lay eggs.

# Amazing survivors

## Who survived?
About 65 million years ago, all the dinosaurs, flying reptiles and giant sea reptiles died out. The animals that lived on were nearly all small.

Here are some of the animals and plants that have survived since the time of the dinosaurs. You may be surprised by how many you know!

## Ancient animals
Sharks are the most ancient large animals of all. Turtles appeared 220 million years ago.

## Good design
Cockroaches have hardly changed their shape in over 300 million years!

## Ruling reptiles

Lizards and snakes are better than most animals at surviving famine. They lived on after the dinosaurs.

## The age of the birds

When dinosaurs walked the Earth, their flying relatives, the pterosaurs, ruled the air. But whatever killed the dinosaurs killed the pterosaurs too.

There were few birds when the pterosaurs lived, but when they died out, the skies were free for the birds to take over.

## Dino food

Some of today's plants grew when dinosaurs lived. All sorts of plant-eating dinosaurs ate ferns. So next time you see a fern, imagine Ankylosaurus eating it!